WELL-INTENTIONED WHITE PEOPLE

Rachel Lynett

BROADWAY PLAY PUBLISHING INC
New York
www.broadwayplaypublishing.com
info@broadwayplaypublishing.com

WELL-INTENTIONED WHITE PEOPLE

First edition: December 2023
I S B N: 979-8-88856-005-1

Book design: Marie Donovan
Page make-up: Adobe InDesign
Typeface: Palatino

WELL-INTENTIONED WHITE PEOPLE received its first professional reading as part of PlayFest at the Orlando Shakespeare Theater, in 2017.

WELL-INTENTIONED WHITE PEOPLE was developed in part through Downstage Left at Stage Left Theatre.

WELL-INTENTIONED WHITE PEOPLE received its world premiere at Barrington Stage Company in 16 August-8 September 2018. The cast and creative contributors were:

CASS .... Myxolydia Tyler
VIV .... Victoria Frings
PARKER .... Samy El-Noury
DEAN WEST .... Andrea Cirie
MARA .... Cathryn Wake

Director .... Tiffany Nichole Greene
Sound Designer .... Joel Abbott
Costume Designer .... Lux Haac
Lighting Designer .... Scott Pinkney
Scenic Designer .... Adam Rigg
Production Stage Manager .... Heather Klein
Casting .... McCorkle Casting Ltd; Pat McCorkle, Katja Zarolinski
Berkshire Press Representative .... Charlie Siedenburg

CHARACTERS & SETTING

CASS, *early to mid 30s, female, Black, college professor*

VIV, *early 30s, female, White,* CASS'*s roommate, "Activist"*

PARKER, *mid 30s, trans man, Latinx, college professor*

DEAN WEST, *50s, female, white, Dean of the Arts Division*

MARA, *mid 20s, female, white, student at the college*

PARKER *must be played by a trans or a masc GNC actor comfortable using he/him pronouns.* PARKER *cannot be played by a woman in drag or a cis man.*

A "hip" and liberal town in a red state (in the United States). Maybe Austin or Orlando or Northwest Arkansas.

NOTES ON STYLE

The missing periods are on purpose. Dashes appear when a character is cut off. A missing period is when a character cuts themselves off.

Moments vs shifts vs pause:

I've been told I write dialogue like a character in a chess game. Intelligent characters constantly having a battle of wits. Leaning into that, I'm attempting to use "moment" and "shift" instead of "beat." For me, a moment is a chance for one or more characters to step back and reassess "the board." It's taking a breath, planning out their next move. It's passive. Shifts are active. It's a character moving a piece, closing in on "the king" of the scene. It's an active play for what they want.

"I must confess that over the last few years I have been gravely disappointed with the white moderate. I have almost reached the regrettable conclusion that the Negro's great stumbling block in the stride toward freedom is not the White Citizen's Council-er or the Ku Klux Klanner, but the white moderate who is more devoted to "order" than to justice."
Martin Luther King, Jr., *Letter from Birmingham Jail*

Scene 1

(Friday night. CASS *sits in her living room, reading a comic book and drinking some scotch. In her living room are half packed boxes all half full of* CASS*'s things.)*

(A moment. Her phone lights up. She ignores it. After a beat or two, VIV *storms in.)*

VIV: Oh my God.

CASS: Hi Viv.

VIV: Cass. Oh my God. Have you seen your car?

CASS: I have.

VIV: How…how long has it said that?

CASS: I guess since after lunch. It wasn't like that when I took a lunch break so after—

VIV: How are you not freaking out?

*(*CASS *unwillingly closes her comic book.)*

CASS: It's a word.

VIV: The worst word.

CASS: It's not the worst word. I will deal with it in the morning.

VIV: Aren't you worried? We need to call the police.

CASS: We do not need to call the police.

VIV: This is a…this is a hate crime.

*(*CASS *shifts.)*

CASS: Viv, I don't want to

I want to finish reading, enjoy the nice scotch I just got, and deal with it in the morning.

VIV: Wait. You drove to the liquor store with it—
(Saying that)

CASS: Viv, it's fine.

VIV: It's completely not fine. Stuff like this isn't supposed to happen in our town. Like I know we're—

CASS: Viv.

VIV: But we don't live in a…things like this don't happen here or at least if they do we don't just do nothing. If you see something, say something. That's how—

CASS: Viv?

VIV: Yes?

CASS: I really, really don't want to talk about this.

VIV: Someone keyed…the n word…on your car today. That is unacceptable, Cass. I'm serious.

CASS: I know.

(Moment)

VIV: I can make the call if that would make you more comfortable.

CASS: It didn't happen to you.

VIV: It happened to us. What's next? We do nothing when they throw a brick through the window? When they burn crosses on our front yard.

CASS: Is there any part of you that understands how ridiculous you're being right now?

VIV: This is dangerous, Cass. We can't ignore this.

CASS: So we call the cops and then that's it? Right? Like we let them handle it.

VIV: Don't you want to talk about it?

CASS: About the n word?

VIV: Cass, don't— Are you okay? Don't you feel… you're looking at me like I'm a crazy person.

CASS: I have already agreed to call the police.

VIV: There's no part of you that feels…unsafe now? Are you okay to go to work tomorrow?

CASS: Tomorrow is Saturday.

VIV: You must be feeling something.

CASS: I'm a little annoyed. I probably have to get a new paint job and that sucks.
But I thought the whole reason we were calling the police was to let them handle it. Why be afraid if a cop is on your side?

VIV: Now you're just being mean.

CASS: I'm just trying to end this conversation.

VIV: Okay, okay. I get not wanting to— What's our action plan?

CASS: Our action plan?

VIV: Yes. We have to do something.

CASS: I am doing something. I'm calling the police. *(She reaches for her phone.)*

VIV: You clearly don't think they'll help.

CASS: No I do not.

VIV: So what's our plan then?

CASS: My plan is to call the police so my roommate chills out and I can go back to reading.

VIV: Comic books do not count as substantial reading.

CASS: And this feels like a really weird time to start that fight.

(Shift)

VIV: But clearly whoever did it knows who you are. What if they followed you home? What if they know where we live?

CASS: I doubt they know where I live.

VIV: They knew your car.

CASS: So what? They're going to hack into the DMV and get my address? Viv!

VIV: No. Not that obviously. But like can't they look up your address on the campus directory?

CASS: My office address.

VIV: My professors had their personal addresses when I was in school.

CASS: Your professors were dumb.

(A moment)

VIV: I can't believe you drove it around town. With it... saying that

CASS: I couldn't exactly leave it at work.

VIV: Did people look at you weird ?

CASS: No more so than they always do.

VIV: Should we tell the campus police too?

CASS: No. Just one kind of officer will be enough I think.

VIV: But it happened on campus.

CASS: By the t ime you're done, I'll be calling the FBI. I'm only calling the city police. Deal?

*(*VIV *makes a weird face that makes* CASS *laugh. This does not make* VIV *happy.)*

VIV: Someone is trying to hurt you.

CASS: By keying my car?

VIV: They damaged your property.

CASS: It's probably some bitter student I gave an F to.

VIV: Some bitter student who knows what car you drive.

CASS: I have a bumper sticker with a quote from Chimamanda Ngozi Adichie. I really don't think it was that hard to guess.

VIV: I told you not to get that bumper sticker.

CASS: Viv. Seriously? *(She reaches for her comic book.)*

VIV: Okay. I wanna see you do it.

CASS: What?

VIV: I wanna see you call the police.

CASS: You're kidding. Right?

VIV: Put them on speaker phone.

*(*CASS *watches* VIV *for a moment.* VIV *stands her ground.* CASS *reaches for her phone again.)*

CASS: *(As she dials)* Fine.

Scene 2

(Later that night, PARKER *and* CASS *sit in* CASS*'s living room, drinking beers.* PARKER *is grading.* CASS *is reading a comic book.)*

PARKER: Viv seemed more uptight than usual. How's her activism work going?

CASS: Last I heard she and her…fuck, what's the new group called…um…anyway, they've got this a fundraiser for "LGBT homeless kids" in the area.

PARKER: That doesn't sound as awful as her last one. The one with—

CASS: But they're literally going to homeless shelters and kind of just asking "hey are you gay? Are you sure? What about you?"

PARKER: Oh.

CASS: Right. And they're not really working with the homeless shelter that already helps that community.

(A moment)

PARKER: She Facebook messaged me.

CASS: Jesus. When?

PARKER: Cass, come on. The cops were just here.

CASS: I only called the cops because of her.

*(*CASS *stops trying to read. And pulls out her phone. She shows* PARKER *the picture.)*

CASS: So you saw my car right?

PARKER: Yeah. They spelled it wrong. Everybody knows that word ends with an "a" now. Even racists listen to rap music.

*(*CASS *reacts to* PARKER *trying to cheer her up. A moment.)*

CASS: I'm kinda worried.

PARKER: Yeah. Maybe it's a good idea to—

CASS: No, not the car. I'm worried about…Viv's next step in her action plan.

PARKER: Her action plan? You worried she'll tell everyone at the next homeowners meeting?

CASS: She might!

PARKER: Viv is "shook". I'll be surprised if she even leaves her room for the next couple of days.

CASS: It didn't happen to her.

PARKER: It's Viv. Everything happens to her. Also, maybe this would be a good time to move out. That way you wouldn't have to worry—

CASS: Parker.

PARKER: You've been packing for months.

CASS: Literally two.

PARKER: That's more than enough time to—

CASS: We just broke up a month ago. I'm not even sure that we're— *(really over)* I want to wait until the semester is over. Just to be…sure.

PARKER: Sure of what?

CASS: Just drop it , alright?

PARKER: You're obviously upset.

CASS: This doesn't feel like something I could keep quiet.

PARKER: Why would you want

CASS: I really don't need bad publicity right now.

PARKER: Bad publici— Oh.

CASS: Yeah.

PARKER: You could get tenure somewhere else.

CASS: Could I?

PARKER: You're still young and obviously—

CASS: Parker.

PARKER: All I'm saying is that it wouldn't be impossible. Get tenure somewhere else.

CASS: I don't want tenure somewhere else. Why else would I have stayed here if I'm not Jesus. I'm published. I've gone to all of those fucking terrible conferences where a bunch of white people literally attempt to explain slavery to me. I deserve to at least know it was for something. And I don't want it to be ruined because my ex girlfriend thinks she's Elizabeth Cady Stanton.

PARKER: I always hated the suffragists. Did you see that quiz where it was like Who said it: a KKK leader or a suffragist? And it was all suffragists.

CASS: Parker.

PARKER: Most people your age don't even get offered tenure.

CASS: I am not most people my age. Most people my age don't have my resume.

PARKER: Wow. Okay.

CASS: I didn't mean
I just don't want this to mess with everything I've worked so hard for.

(Shift)

PARKER: Honestly, if anything, the college will love this.

CASS: What?

PARKER: You're just going to have to cooperate. Put on a big smile, show the white people you care about racism just as much but not more than they do, and just kind of roll with it.

CASS: So, it could be nothing then. Right? Like I don't have to go on the news or anything?

PARKER: You may just have to deal with an annoying email about how welcoming we are as a campus and how we do not tolerate hate speech. Just smile, nod, it'll be done with.

CASS: Is that how your last college handled your transition?

PARKER: No.

CASS: Parker.

PARKER: This isn't the same thing, Cass. It's an…attack. And people sorta love this shit. They love a chance to rally behind a person of color and plan protests and marches and talk about how they understand what microaggression is now.
Protesting is the new "brunch" for white people.

(Moment)

CASS: Don't you sometimes wish that we worked in like…Louisiana? Or like the "rough" parts of this state? Where people are homophobic and racist and the challenge is educating people.
I just feel like it's either blatantly racist people or the safe space, safety-pin wearing "I don't see color" people.
I would rather the racist people.

PARKER: The safety pin people aren't the people who were doing the lynchings.

CASS: No. They were just the people who let it happen.

PARKER: Maybe you should take a few days off work.

CASS: I'm fine.

PARKER: It just happened. Maybe now's a good time to take a breath and—

CASS: The damage wasn't permanent. It's nothing. I'm not going to give someone the power to affect my life over something so trivial.

PARKER: You're not acting like it's trivial.

CASS: I'm not freaked out because it happened. I'm freaked out because//

PARKER: Tenure, I know.

CASS: //I have a legit legacy. The second this gets out no one is going to care that I was the keynote at four different conferences this year. Even if I did leave the college, all of my interviews would be about this. This stupid, stupid incident that in the grand scheme of my life is meaningless.

PARKER: What if it escalates?

CASS: Please don't do this. I already have to worry about Viv. I can't worry about you too.

(Moment)

PARKER: Well what are you going to do about your car? Can I at least take it to the shop so you don't have to?

CASS: Yeah. Sure. Fine. Thanks.

*(*PARKER *nods and goes back to grading.* CASS *drinks.)*

Scene 3

(Monday morning. CASS *struggles to get into her office while dialing on the phone and holding a newspaper.)*

CASS: *(As soon as it stops ringing; on the phone)* In what fucking world did you think I'd be okay with this?

(The door opens. In a separate space, VIV *comes on stage.)*

VIV: Cass? Hi. Oh—I—I didn't do it.

CASS: So walk me through this, Viv. Honestly. How exactly did this happen if you didn't do it? "Oh hey sis. I'm stressed and sad so let me share this super personal story that isn't mine."

VIV: Cass. That isn't what happened. I didn't think Gemma would— *(Put it in the paper)*

CASS: *(Still doing her* VIV *voice)* "Oh. You're going to write about it in the paper? That would be amazing."

VIV: I begged her not to tell anyone. I told her I was coming to her as a sister. She's the only family I have in town. I didn't think she'd

CASS: She's a reporter. It's literally her job.

VIV: She's my sister! I thought I could trust her.

CASS: Why? Why would you think that?

VIV: Cass. I didn't do this.

(In the distance, there's a clicking sound.)

CASS: Dammit.

(It's the sound of heels hitting the tile. Hard. Someone's coming.)

CASS: I have to go. Really. I am one hundred percent not okay with this and I will yell about this some more when I get home tonight.

*(*CASS *hangs up before* VIV *can say anything.* VIV *leaves the stage.)*

*(*CASS *sits down at her desk, skims the newspaper again, and stress eats carrots from her briefcase. The sound of heels is closer now.)*

(There's a knock on her door.)

CASS: Come in.

(The door opens. DEAN WEST *walks in and sits down.* CASS *sets her carrots down and tries to clean up her desk.)*

CASS: Hi. How are you Dean West? *(She thinks about hiding the newspaper but there's really no point.)*

DEAN WEST: I'm well.

CASS: Great. That's—

DEAN WEST: How are you?

CASS: I'm…I'm okay.

DEAN WEST: I saw a note on your door. You're canceling office hours?

CASS: Just for the morning. Yes. I got behind on some grading and I—

DEAN WEST: I read the paper this morning. Have you read the paper this morning? Cover page. Continues on page 4.

(CASS looks down at the paper on her desk. Is there any way she can lie about not having seen the article?)

DEAN WEST: Professor Davis?

CASS: I was actually just getting to—

DEAN WEST: There's an article about a college professor being assaulted on our campus.

CASS: Dean West—

DEAN WEST: The author of the piece, a Gemma Wilde, didn't name the professor. Isn't your partner's last name also Wilde?

CASS: Oh. Actually— *(Viv isn't my)*

DEAN WEST: Well, Gemma…Wilde mentioned the professor works here, included a picture of the vehicle, and mentions that said professor specializes in the literature and art of the African diaspora, specifically looking at the Caribbean.

Professor Davis!

CASS: Dean West, I— Yes, I'm the unnamed professor in the article. I'm aware my colleagues know this. I'm aware my students know this. If there's something you'd like for me to do, please just tell me what it is.

(Moment. There's a change in DEAN WEST.*)*

DEAN WEST: Why didn't you come to us first?

CASS: I didn't come…I didn't go to anyone. I just drove home. And tried to deal with it. But then my roommate called a reporter and everything just spiraled. I didn't give my consent for any of this to be written about me. And I'd love to call a lawyer and sue the hell out of the paper but that's not going to make everyone unread it.

So…is there any action I need to take now? Anything the university needs me to do?

(Another moment)

DEAN WEST: Are you okay?

CASS: Vexed but okay.

DEAN WEST: Are you sure you're okay?

CASS: Yes.

DEAN WEST: Okay. The president has asked that we not make this into a scandal.

CASS: Great. I don't want—

DEAN WEST: But I found that really irritating. Like how dare he?

(CASS's face goes blank. Where is this going?)

DEAN WEST: To do nothing means we allow this sort of behavior. And that's not the message I want to send our students or staff. It's definitely not the message I want to send to you after an attack like this.//

CASS: Right but—

DEAN WEST: //So I started thinking. What can we do? How do we send the right message to our students so that they know this is a safe environment?

CASS: //Well, we have resources for--//

DEAN WEST: And so I thought it would be amazing to start an annual, "we will not allow discrimination" event. And I tried to figure out who would be perfect for it. And it's you. Especially now.

CASS: Why would I be perfect?

DEAN WEST: You'd be able to speak from experience, Professor Davis. The students need to see a face they recognize. It'd be a special campus wide event. We could address latent racism and homophobia and our personal responsibility to stand together.

CASS: Homophobia?

DEAN WEST: Yes, of course.

CASS: Okay. Well, great. I'll prepare a speech about—

DEAN WEST: Oh. No. Not just a speech.

(A moment)

CASS: Dean West, I don't have time to plan an entire event. It's almost—

DEAN WEST: *(Thinking aloud and very proud of herself)* Under this administration, where the country is headed, we really need to show our students we aren't afraid to stand up to this hatred. That our own faculty has been assaulted and we will not be silent. I want it to be a fundraiser. Put together a list of organizations that help with fighting injustice. Like the ACLU or NAACP. We can donate the funds to them. And show we're on the right side of history.

(Pause. DEAN WEST *waits for an excited reaction from* CASS. CASS *tries her best to smile.)*

CASS: So. Just so I'm clear. I'm putting together a list of all the organizations that help with fighting racism and homophobia and…

DEAN WEST: It's so much more than just a list. It's raising up our community

CASS: Dean West, it's almost finals. Do you really— *(think there's time for this?)*

DEAN WEST: Our students need this, Professor Davis. Could you prepare a quick packet of the three organizations you choose with descriptions on what they do, who they help. Let's say by the end of the day.

*(*CASS *stares blankly at* DEAN WEST.*)*

DEAN WEST: Any injustice really. Maybe Planned Parenthood, NAACP, and maybe the NCLR, whatever they're called now. Unidos something. Oh! You're close to Professor Jimenez, right? Maybe you two could work together on this. *(She checks the time.)* I really need to go. Update me by the end of the day with your list. It doesn't have to be those organizations. Any that you feel you connect to. But please keep the list diverse. I can't wait to hear it.

*(*DEAN WEST *leaves.* CASS *reaches for the newspaper and looks at it again.)*

CASS: *(Under her breath)* Shit. *(She lifts her head and grabs her office phone. She dials a number and puts it on speaker.)*

PARKER: *(Off stage and through the speaker)* Yo. I'm down for a quick pity party but I have class in thirty.

CASS: Seriously?

PARKER: It's one article, Cass. It doesn't even mention your name.

CASS: There's a picture of my car.

PARKER: It could be worse, Cass.

(Moment)

CASS: Dean West wants us to plan Equality Day. Hello? Are you still—

PARKER: Us?

CASS: Us.

PARKER: The fuck is Equality Day?

CASS: It's the part where I nod and smile. And just go with it.

PARKER: Why do I have to?

CASS: I think you're the first other brown person she thought of.

PARKER: I hate white people.

Scene 4

(That evening, CASS, PARKER, *and* VIV *sit in the living room of* CASS *and* VIV*'s home. It's tense. There are papers everywhere.* CASS *is flipping through, trying to make sense of it all.* PARKER *is just watching* VIV. *After a moment or two,* CASS *acknowledges the tension.)*

CASS: Viv, you really don't have to be here. I know you're probably busy with planning your own fundraiser so—

VIV: I would just like to say, again, that if the college really wants to support the community, they'd give to local charities, not national ones.

PARKER: You mean like yours?

VIV: We're a nonprofit, not a charity. But yes. Helps us rebuild the community//

CASS: //Guys//

PARKER: How exactly does your nonprofit help people? //

CASS: //Parker //

VIV: I'm happy you asked. Again. We provide food to the homeless, we help prep them for job interviews, we wash their clothes. We //

CASS: //Viv //

VIV: //We even work with jobs around town to help with job placement. Just today I got two people hired.

PARKER: Yeah? Where?

CASS: *(Mostly under her breath)* //Jesus. //

VIV: // These people have serious brain…they're not okay. It's not like I'm going to be able to get them a job at a bank or some firm. //

PARKER: So dishes then?

VIV: I didn't say dishes. Would you really want someone with severe PTSD attempting to deliver a baby? What do you exp ect will—

CASS: Guys! Viv, we haven't decided where the money will go yet. I gave Dean West five options and two of them were local. It's her choice now. Okay? It's a bullshit event that probably won't raise a ton of money. It literally just exists to make the college feel like they did something special to get recruitment numbers up.

VIV: If you think it's a bullshit event, you're going to plan it that way. This event, regardless of the reason of conception, could be really big for this area. People need to know—

CASS: I know, I know. I heard the spiel. *(To* PARKER*)* Can you chill?

PARKER: Yeah. Sorry.

CASS: I have no idea how to make sense of all this stuff. I handed her my list and then she handed me back all of this

*(*CASS *motions to the papers.* VIV *picks up some of the papers.)*

VIV: This is a Tedtalk. Like the transcript of

CASS: I know.

PARKER: Did she just research all afternoon?

CASS: Yes. She did. And she wants it to be a two day event. And she wants us to cover racism, immigration, LGBT+ rights, and the refugee crisis. She wants racism and queer rights one day and refugee and immigration stuff the next day.

VIV: That makes sense. They're related.

(PARKER shoots CASS a look. CASS ignores it.)

CASS: The problem is she wants all of this to happen before finals.

PARKER: That's too fast a turn around.

CASS: Not to her . So we need available speakers who can be here quickly. And create a schedule that somehow fits within the college schedule....

PARKER: Are we not going to take a minute to acknowledge how fucked up this is?

CASS: Parker.

PARKER: They're making the person who was attacked//

CASS: //I wasn't attacked

PARKER: //Plan a whole event to make them feel better.

VIV: It's not about making people feel better. It's about raising awareness.

PARKER: It's a weak and transparent attempt to do literally nothing while the oppressed people do all the work. Did Dean West even ask you if you wanted this? Or did she just tell you?

VIV: And if they didn't ask Cass to do it, you'd say they were silencing her.

PARKER: Are you seri—

CASS: This isn't about awareness. It isn't about oppressed people. I'm literally doing this for tenure.

(Moment)

VIV: I can talk to Stacey. See if she can find someone willing to be a speaker. She's still got some contacts from her work with the ACLU.

CASS: Great. Thanks.

(Shift)

PARKER: You're going to address the campus right?

CASS: What?

PARKER: You're planning on saying something right?

CASS: God, no.

PARKER: Don't you think you should?

VIV: This event is only happening as a reaction to what happened to you. So…you should prepare something. It makes sense.

CASS: And say what? It really sucks to be a black person?

PARKER: What it means to be queer and black and teaching spoiled liberal white kids that they're still privileged.

CASS: I hate the word queer.
This had nothing to do with who I sleep with. It's racially motivated. Let's not turn this into—

PARKER: Your students read the paper too. They know that whatever happens next, it's because of what happened to you.

CASS: I can't get my students to read the homework assignment. I doubt they've read the paper. I spent an hour talking about who Rachel Dolezal was and I think they still don't know.

PARKER: And it would look good for tenure. If you were the keynote.

CASS: What?

PARKER: It shows you believe in the same message the college does. And that you support their ideals. Like-minded folks and such. It's not like you don't talk about this stuff all the time.

CASS: I don't talk about it in a personal way. I talk about slavery and its aftermath and failed reconstruction. I don't talk about my…me. I don't talk about me.

PARKER: Not even in class? As an example of prevalent racism?

CASS: So what exactly am I supposed to say? Whoever did this is probably not planning on attending Equality Day.

PARKER: Luckily for us, we're not doing it for that person.

VIV: How do you know that person won't come?

(PARKER *send another look to* CASS.)

CASS: Viv, I know you deeply believe singing kumbiya and public marches and protest days are going to solve the world's problems.

VIV: *(Mostly to herself)* You can be so incredibly condescending. All I'm saying is that—

CASS: And I'm just saying, as I've always said, you know who doesn't show up for the women's march? The women you're marching for. The only women who can even afford to march aren't typically the ones who—

PARKER: Let's not do it.

CASS: What?

PARKER: Let's say no. Like you should've. Right away. You're right. This isn't about educating racists. It's about making "liberals" comfortable. Neither one of us supports that.

CASS: Tenure. Supporting the message of the campus. Uniting with faculty. TENURE. Remember? Dean West is on the goddamn committee. I can't just be like "Hey

Dean West. You're what's wrong with the country. You're why Trump got elected." They will fire me.

VIV: They can't fire you for that.

(PARKER sends another look to CASS.)

CASS: I'll be the stupid keynote. And talk about how awesome it is to be a black queer woman at an almost all white college. Yay.

(Shift)

VIV: What if this is the moment where we can educate the educated? I know you think that these things are always for the super privileged but what if we turn that and use it to our advantage?

PARKER: There is no our, Viv.

VIV: Cass. You're always talking about how being an ally and saying you're an ally isn't the same thing.

CASS: Because it's not.

VIV: Well maybe this is the time for you to exp lain how to be a real ally and not just someone who uses social media as a glory badge.

CASS: You mean like I did for you? *(Moment)* Viv, wait. I'm not—
People don't want to hear about how what they're doing is superficial. People don't want to hear there's nothing to do because it's too fucking late. This event is not going to erase the fact that someone keyed…the n word…into my car. Nor will it stop that person from doing something worse. Reacting after tragedy does nothing. It's too late.
I can't give a speech that says "sucks to suck, assholes. You were too late. But thanks for your crap attempt to show me you care." No one cares when it's inconvenient. You think any of these people would've stopped the person who wrote it?

VIV: Yes I do. I would've. And believing no one would help is a horrible way to look at the world. *(Shift. She leaves.)*

CASS: So if I'm the keynote who else do we get?

PARKER: There was that student a couple of weeks ago who had to be escorted to class because she was attacked for wearing a hijab.

CASS: No, not her.

PARKER: She was all over the school paper.

CASS: She was wearing it "in solidarity."

PARKER: The college really likes how brave she is.

CASS: She's white!

PARKER: We're going to need white people up there anyway.

CASS: Are you…she's white. And is known for

PARKER: This is the part where we, despite our better judgement, smile and nod.

CASS: Parker.

PARKER: Smiling and nodding, Cass.

Scene 5

(CASS sits in her office, looking at a school newspaper from six months ago. MARA is on the cover page. CASS gets out a lighter and considers burning the newspaper. There's a knock on the door.)

CASS: Yeah. Come in.

(MARA enters.)

MARA: Hi Professor Davis.

CASS: Hello Mara. Sit down.

*(*MARA *sits down.)*

MARA: I'm actually really happy you called me into your office. I've been trying to get into your African art class but my advisor said I have to take—

CASS: Mara.

MARA: Yes Professor Davis?

CASS: It's actually Doc— Just Cass. Call me Cass

And you have to take Intro to the African Diaspora with Dr. Greene first. I can't change that.

MARA: But I've already—

CASS: Anyway, we're…the college is planning an Equality Day.

MARA: Oh?

CASS: And we were wondering if you could speak about your experience. When you were wearing a hijab in solidarity.

MARA: You mean when a student called me Muslim scum?

CASS: Yes.

MARA: I can't believe all he got was a suspension. What kind of message are we sending—

CASS: Mara.

MARA: Yes?

CASS: I'm just curious. Are you Muslim?

MARA: Catholic. But Mother Teresa said "If we have no peace, it is because we have forgotten that we belong to each other."

*(*CASS *doesn't know how to respond. A moment)*

CASS: Right. Um…we were wondering if you would like to prepare a speech about your solidarity and the refugee crisis. Aren't you organizing…something on campus right now anyway?

MARA: Yes. We're working with Blue Unity, that group on campus for religious parties to—

CASS: Yup. I know about them.

MARA: Right. Well we're working together to see if we can get a structure built for incoming refugees. So we're raising money to—

CASS: That's great. Maybe you could work wit h Blue Unity to create a presentation then? Equality Day is coming up soon so if it's too much work…

MARA: When is it?

CASS: Dean West would really like to have it within the next two weeks. So next week Friday?

MARA: That sounds great. I could get catering to do food from all over the world as part of the event.

CASS: Great.

MARA: We could have pupusas, sushi, um…pad thai, curry

CASS: Mara.

MARA: Yes?

CASS: That all sounds really great. I need to…get back to work so um…

MARA: Could I ask you a question?

CASS: Sure.

MARA: When that person keyed your car and wrote the word nigger, what was your first response?

(CASS *stares at* MARA. *Is this really happening?)*

MARA: Was it to, like, scream? Did you cry? Did you call your boyfriend? Husband? Partner?

CASS: Mara, I—

MARA: Have you ever been called a nigger before? Was it the first t ime? Did you grow up in a racially divided city? Or was it like here where everyone basically got along?

CASS: I'm not sure we should—

MARA: What were your parents like? I Google-d you and it says both of your parents are from the Caribbean. Like, they're immigrants. You're actually first generation. How does that play into your identity? Is your relationship with that word different because you're not really "African American"?

CASS: What's happening?

MARA: I'm interviewing you.

CASS: Why?

MARA: For the school paper.

CASS: Since when do you work for the school paper?

MARA: Well after my incident I wanted to get involved so I contacted the—

CASS: Yeah, okay okay. And were you going to ask me for my consent to be interviewed?

MARA: I'm sorry Professor Cass. I thought—

CASS: Just Cass.

MARA: I thought you'd be willing to do it. Because you're planning Equality Day. So I figured you'd be open to discourse.

*(*CASS *is at a loss of words. Again)*

MARA: This is an incredibly important conversation. Don't you think so?

*(*CASS *hesitantly nods.)*

MARA: And who better to lead the conversation than a professor who has a PhD in slave studies.

CASS: My PhD is in Comparative US History with a focus on—

MARA: That's essentially what studying the diaspora is though right? Studying the traffic of slavery?

CASS: No. Not exactly.

MARA: I mean, you're obviously interested in it because of your parents.

CASS: My parents?

MARA: Your dad is from Haiti.

CASS: I know where—

MARA: That was a major port for the slave trade. Surely, he must have ancestors who worked in the Caribbean. That must've impacted you. And if it didn't, okay. That's what I'm here for. I want the student body to know about you. And how you work.

CASS: How I work?

MARA: Like what makes you tick. What brought you to the African diaspora? Why not the Irish diaspora?

(CASS searches the office. She's not exactly looking for an escape but she's definitely looking for a distraction.)

CASS: Mara, I really need to get back to grading papers.

MARA: Dean West thinks this profile is a great idea.

CASS: You talked to Dean West?

MARA: She gave me the idea for it.

CASS: Dean West asked you to do a profile on me?

MARA: Yeah. She floated the idea but

CASS: Did she say "Profile Professor Davis"?

MARA: No. She said, "Professor Davis is having a rough time and we need to show her the college supports her" and something about how the paper should do a small write up about on campus racism.

CASS: Right.

MARA: I just think it's really interesting, you know? I'm from the south, like the real south, and we have such a history of dealing with this. I think it makes us more…I don't know…emotionally available and honest when it comes to how we treat people who look different than us. It's nuts isn't it? We're all one race. The human race. I've got a cousin who is honest to God your complexion and everyone just—

CASS: Mara, you— Is there another time we could have this conversation?

MARA: Oh for sure. If it's easier for you, I could just email you the questions and you could answer them later. When you're ready.

*(*CASS *nods slowly.)*

CASS: Yes, that sounds great.

MARA: I hate that this happened to you, profes— Cass.

CASS: Yeah. Me too.

MARA: I'm excited about Equality Day, though. A step in the right direction.

CASS: I certainly hope so.

MARA: Can I ask one more question?

*(*CASS *shrugs. Is there really any stopping her?* MARA *stares at* CASS*. Oh right. She's waiting for affirmative consent.)*

CASS: Yes, Mara. Ask away.

MARA: Do you think that if you were darker skinned the attack would've been more violent?

CASS: I…I'm not exactly— *(Light-skinned)*

MARA: Or if you were a male? We just started talking about complexion politics in my gender studies class and—

CASS: Mara, I really need you to
Leave my office. Right now. Please.

MARA: Right. Sorry. Okay. Thanks prof— Thanks Cass.
(She leaves the office.)

Scene 6

(Later that day. CASS *is reading one of her textbooks and preparing a lecture in a classroom.)*

(She's avoiding her office.)

(She hears the sound of heels clacking hard against tile.)

CASS: Well shit.

(The door opens. DEAN WEST *walks in.)*

DEAN WEST: Afternoon Professor Davis.

CASS: *(Without looking up)* Hello Dean West.

DEAN WEST: I was surprised you weren't in your office.

CASS: I wanted a change. Thought I'd be more focused in—

DEAN WEST: How's Equality Day going?

CASS: Great. It should be really effective.

DEAN WEST: Wonderful.
A student came into my office today.

*(*CASS *expects* DEAN WEST *to say something else. She doesn't.)*

CASS: Okay.

DEAN WEST: She wanted to file a complaint.

(This day is seriously not getting better.)

CASS: Against? Was it another racist incident or

DEAN WEST: No. A complaint against you.

CASS: Right. Of course. Mara?

DEAN WEST: She was uncomfortable with you asking her if she's Muslim or not. And thought once she said she was Catholic, you were…indignant. Her word, not mine. I actually don't think that's the right word for what she was trying to explain. She said you refused to do a profile with her and kicked her out of your office because of her…background.

CASS: She thinks I don't want her to profile me because she's Catholic?

DEAN WEST: No. Because she's white. She called you exclusionary. Also her word. That you supposedly show special preference to the African American students. And that had she been African American, she's sure you would've done the profile And something about you not lett ing her in your class. It was all coming very fast. And was hard to keep up with.

CASS: Dean West.

DEAN WEST: The thesis of her argument, I think, was that the only reason she isn't in your class is because she's white.

CASS: She hasn't taken the prerequisite course.

DEAN WEST: Professor Davis, it's Mara. I'm not here to defend her. Mara's constantly filing complaints. She filed a complaint when we were observing Columbus Day and still calling it Columbus Day.

CASS: Right. So then—

DEAN WEST: This is the reason we really need Equality Day. Students feel tense and people are choosing sides. We need to show people the only side is the side that stands with the oppressed.

Having Mara speak is a good idea. If she's on stage, she won't be in the audience booing. Plus she can mobilize a lot of students.

CASS: Yeah.

(Shift)

DEAN WEST: Also. I would like for you to let her into your class.

CASS: Dean West, she's not—

DEAN WEST: Because now is not the time for protests.

CASS: Protests?

DEAN WEST: You don't have to pass her. Just override her in. If you're lucky she'll realize she's too far behind and will drop the class. Or she'll have to risk her 4.0 which we both know she won't do.

CASS: So we're really going to let Mara bully us into—

DEAN WEST: We don't need this to turn into an… incident. Equality Day should be celebrated. Not… dragged down by allegedly racist professors.

CASS: Racist profe—

DEAN WEST: She's not the only white student to make a complaint about you.

CASS: People tend to get upset when their privilege is called into question.

DEAN WEST: Yes. Probably. But also, I think it's sometimes hard to remember that not all white people have that privilege. Some of your students, your white students, have no privilege at all.
It isn't the end of the world, Professor Davis. It's a compromise made with good intentions to improve race relations here on campus. A tiny, tiny step. Mara is not the rich, spoiled girl you've painted her to be. Did you know she was in foster care until she was thirteen? That's not exactly a privileged life.

CASS: That's not how privilege works.

DEAN WEST: We need to stand united right now, Professor Davis. The college depends on our professors to set an example for our students and I just want you to be mindful of the example you are setting, consciously or not.

CASS: My job, as an educator, is to ensure that my students have a—

DEAN WEST: Yes. And you're doing a great job of that. I genuinely look forward to discussing it in your tenure review.

(Moment)

CASS: Okay. Yes. You're right. I will override her in. Anything else?

DEAN WEST: I love that you're giving a speech. I think that's a nice touch.

CASS: Thanks.

(A moment)

DEAN WEST: I also wanted to let you know. Due to the circumstances, we're pushing back your tenure interview until the Friday after Equality Day.

CASS: The circumstances?

DEAN WEST: Equality Day. Mara. We want to make sure we approach it with clear minds.

CASS: Makes sense. Thanks for letting me know.

DEAN WEST: Tension is high. We just don't want to—

CASS: I understand. *(She returns to reading and preparing.)*

DEAN WEST: You seem tense.

CASS: Just busy.

DEAN WEST: Sure.

(Pause. CASS *expects* DEAN WEST *to leave.* DEAN WEST *doesn't. They both sit in silence while* CASS *reads and* DEAN WEST *just waits.)*

DEAN WEST: I understand how…political Equality Day might seem but I honestly believe it's important.

CASS: Yes, I agree.

DEAN WEST: And it could drastically change the reality so many students are facing. We could help create an honest and safe space. And maybe a festival isn't the perfect way to do it but it's at least a start. We have to start somewhere, don't we? *(A moment)* It's all a bit ridiculous, though isn't it?

CASS: I…um

DEAN WEST: Didn't my parents already march for this? Sometimes I look around and think how are we still here?

CASS: Yeah.

DEAN WEST: How many times do we need to say stop killing black people? Maybe there should just be a constant, daily email reminder that every time something racist happens, every Black person gets twenty dollars added in their bank account.

CASS: I'd be so rich.

DEAN WEST: The country would go bankrupt.

*(*CASS *and* DEAN WEST *both enjoy the moment.)*

DEAN WEST: I understand it's a little absurd. Trust me. I do.
But, unfortunately, the college does actually need this.
The president of the university tried to tell me we're still post-racial with a couple outliers and I—
This event is desperately needed.

*(*CASS *nods.)*

DEAN WEST: I thank God every day I went to Howard University for a semester. White people just don't get it.
I really had my eyes opened. I understand the struggle. How traumatizing this must be for you. I would be beside myself if I came to my car and the word nigger was on it.

*(*CASS *tries to process what's happened. Moment)*

CASS: I appreciate for your concern and support, Dean West. I'm okay. I'm thankful I work at such a supportive college and can't wait to get Equality Day launched. I think it will be very great for the college.

DEAN WEST: The college stands behind you, Professor Davis. If you need anything, please just let us know. We're here for you.

CASS: Yes. I feel very supported right now. Thanks.

DEAN WEST: You're welcome.

*(*DEAN WEST *leaves.* CASS *knocks the papers off of her desk.)*

Scene 7

*(*CASS *is at home, drinking bourbon directly from the bottle. She's just gotten home from work and does not look like she had a good day.* VIV *walks in and sees* CASS*. She sets her bag down and sits next to* CASS*.* CASS *puts her legs on top of* VIV*'s or something intimate and similar.)*

VIV: Good day?

*(*CASS *nods.)*

CASS: Unbelievably good.

VIV: Me too.

*(*VIV *extends her arm for the bottle.* CASS *passes it.)*

CASS: A student filed a complaint against me.

VIV: For what?

CASS: Discrimination. She thinks I don't like her because she's white.

VIV: Oh.

CASS: Oh?

VIV: I'm not saying she's justified.

CASS: You also aren't saying she's not.

VIV: I don't think...I don't know enough about what happened but I don't think you're prejudiced against white people in general

CASS: What?

VIV: But I think you have a complicated relationship with white women.

*(*CASS *moves her legs, takes the bottle back and drinks.)*

(Moment)

CASS: Why was your day shitty?

VIV: You don't want to know why— *(I think that)*

CASS: Not really. No I don't. I want to pretend like you didn't say it because I've had the worst day and don't feel like yelling right now. Because if I start, I will not stop.

VIV: You broke up with me because I was white.

CASS: I broke up with you because you are the epitome of the problem.

VIV: I didn't choose to be white, Cass. And how am I the problem when I've dedicated my life to—

CASS: Viv. I really, really don't want to do this.

VIV: I get it. I think life conditions you to feel a certain way and you don't know how to shake it. So you look at me trying to help but you don't know how disassociate me from the general, very academic idea of "white women." I'm just another Becky to you.

(Shift)

CASS: You are constantly trying to tell me about how I was conditioned. And when something not so great happened to me, you made it all about you. //

VIV: What?

CASS: //I didn't want the police involved. I didn't want Gemma involved. And now I have to plan a whole stupid awareness day and I have to let a psychopath into my class. All because you wanted "to do something."

VIV: People who do nothing—

CASS: And then you talk like you're speaking in quotes.

Viv, it's okay that you come from a rich family. It's okay that you live in a mostly white city. But no not-white person in this city thought racism didn't exist here. It's like you need me to tell you it's okay to be white.

VIV: That's unfair.

CASS: This wasn't about you. None of it was. And yet, somehow, here we are.

(CASS and VIV both sit in silence.)

VIV: I was scared.

CASS: What?

VIV: And so I reacted to that fear. I...I thought "Oh no what if they come here? And something happens to me too?"

(CASS takes a gulp of the bourbon.)

CASS: Well that's shitty.

VIV: You won't even…that's it? That's shitty? At least I'm trying to be honest. I realize—

(There's a knock on the door that interrupts VIV. *Neither* CASS *or* VIV *say anything. The door opens and* PARKER *peeks through.)*

PARKER: Apparently white people were extra horrible today, so I brought gifts. May I come in?

*(*CASS *smiles.* VIV *stands up.)*

VIV: I'll head upstairs.

*(*PARKER *comes into the house holding a six pack.* VIV *heads upstairs.* PARKER *joins* CASS *on the couch.)*

PARKER: It's tense.

CASS: It's always tense.

PARKER: Can we talk about some ways to make it not tense?

CASS: Parker.

PARKER: Because moving in with me is a standing offer.

CASS: Parker.

PARKER: It's just a way out. And it wouldn't be a big move.
You could stay with me until the semester ends and then make the big move—

CASS: But that's still technically moving and I want to wait.

PARKER: Living with Viv still obviously isn't—

CASS: It's not your problem, Parker.

(A moment)

PARKER: I heard about Mara.

CASS: She called me racist. Can you believe—

PARKER: Did you know her real name is Katherine? I'm not even kidding.

CASS: Why do we call her Mara?

PARKER: Weird foster care thing. She didn't want--and I am not kidding she actually calls it this— she didn't want her "slave name."

CASS: Are you fucking serious?

(PARKER *nods.)*

PARKER: Her name is Katherine Elizabeth Blaine. She still hasn't officially changed it.

CASS: Her name on my syllabus is Mara Chigozie.

PARKER: She petitioned the president and

CASS: Right. Of course she did. All she needs now is tanning lotion and dreads.

PARKER: I'm pretty much expecting it. Like any day now she'll start talking about how she's trans- racial.

(Moment)

CASS: It's almost over right? Like all of it.

PARKER: Almost.

CASS: All I have to do now is give a speech, shake some hands, and then…bam…tenure.

PARKER: Have you written it?

CASS: No. I was thinking about winging it. Bullshitting isn't that hard.

PARKER: What happens if you go through all of this and they don't give you tenure?

CASS: What?

PARKER: Have you…considered that?

CASS: Why would they not give me…what do you know?

PARKER: I just know that sometimes things don't go the way we want them to.

(CASS tenses up. Pause. It's a tense pause.)

PARKER: Look. I don't know how relevant it is but they're interviewing a friend of mine from my old college.

CASS: A friend of yours?

PARKER: She's an artist. She's Black. And…

CASS: And she also studies diasporic literature.

PARKER: And she's trans.

CASS: There are no openings at the college right now.

PARKER: So, we knew to keep up appearances, they'd at least attempt a nation-wide search. I mean they always do that to kind of get the fire under—

CASS: Yeah. I know. But that's always just for show. They don't actually interview people unless

PARKER: Unless they decided they wouldn't have to offer anyone tenure. They could just get an adjunct and just postpone it all for seven years. Maybe even— *(never offer tenure)*

CASS: This is such bullshit.

PARKER: Yeah. So maybe don't do this just for the college? Maybe take some time to deal with what actually happened to you.

(CASS reaches for a beer but doesn't move to open it.)

CASS: You know, I always thought I was like the diversity gold star. I'm Black, I'm happily situated under the rainbow, almost all of my relationships have been interracial

PARKER: Why would you want to be a diversity gold star?

CASS: Because that's apparently the only way to not get fucking fired. Now, I'm just ordinary. Black people are the usual. Now I need to be trans for anyone to give a shit about me.

(PARKER shifts.)

CASS: I'm sorry. I didn't...I'm sorry. I didn't mean that.

PARKER: You did. But it's fine. You're upset. Possibly drunk.

CASS: Parker, seriously. I'm—

PARKER: Let it go, Cass.

(Moment)

CASS: The officer called back. Said he had no leads on who did it. And for now they were closing the case. Not enough evidence.
I keep waiting to walk to my car with the window broken into or my tires slashed. But then I'm like would that be the worst thing? It's just a car.

PARKER: Cass.

CASS: I keep thinking. What's the thing that'll scare me? In high school, just seeing that word made me...I don't know...sick. Now I'm just annoyed. I'm not even all that concerned for my safety. I'm so...accepting of it. Is that what's supposed to happen? Enough racist things happen that you just shut down?
I'm waiting for the moment where it clicks in.
Like that moment where you're like "Oh right, this is unacceptable behavior." But it's exp ected at this point.
I don't want to live this way. Do you? And it feels like...fuck...it feels like anytime I do reach out and admit that I'm not okay, it becomes a spectacle. Like a game of who can care the most. It isn't about....

PARKER: Cass. What's going on?

(Moment)

*(*CASS *hands* PARKER *the piece of paper.* PARKER *unfolds it and reads it.)*

CASS: It…it's so much more than just a car, Parker.

PARKER: *(Reading)* Cass. What do you— Go back to Africa.
Cass. What's going on?

CASS: So like two months ago, I started getting these notes. I didn't say anything because it seemed…not worth it I guess?
That's one of the nicer ones by the way.

PARKER: One of the nicer ones?

*(*CASS *reaches for her briefcase. She pulls out a couple of bunched up pieces of paper.)*

*(*PARKER *looks at* CASS *and then begins to read the papers one by one.)*

PARKER: Cass.

CASS: I know

PARKER: So. Jesus. So basically first someone sent you notes. Then you ignored it. Then they scratched your car. Cass…holy shit. I don't even get this much hate mail.

CASS: But you do get some?

PARKER: Yeah but—

CASS: And you hadn't told anyone? We're not having a fucking Equality Day for you.

PARKER: What I got was minor.

CASS: This is minor.

PARKER: No, it's not. It's escalating. Cass, whoever is targeting you wants to send a message. Please tell me you told the cops about this.

*(*CASS *doens't say anything.)*

PARKER: Cass!

CASS: Shh! Viv will hear you. And I'm really not in the mood to talk about how I've been conditioned as a black person.

(PARKER is visibly hurt by CASS wanting to hide this.)

PARKER: You should've told me.

CASS: It's nothing.

CASS: I don't want to make a big deal out of this.

PARKER: It's a big fucking deal!

CASS: Look what happened when a newspaper article was written about my car. A newspaper article I didn't even want written. How do you think Dean West will handle this?

PARKER: At least tell the police.

CASS: For what? For a half-assed police report? What are they going to do? Run a handwriting anaylsis of every student I've had in the last--what--three years?

PARKER: Cass.

CASS: Look me in the eye right now and tell me you trust the police. All of them. That when you get pulled over, your heart doesn't drop. That you don't send a quick text to someone you love. That you know for sure with no doubt in your mind that you'll be able to drive away after the encounter. That you'll be alive.

(PARKER doesn't say anything.)

CASS: Exactly. I'm not calling the police.

PARKER: What if it escalates? Even more than it obviously has. Cass, this serious. You need to—

CASS: We're done talking about it, okay? I'm fine. It's fine.

Scene 8

(The next morning, VIV *is in the kitchen, playing Banana Grams by herself and drinking coffee.* PARKER *walks into the kitchen and hovers for a moment in the background. And then:)*

PARKER: Is Cass still asleep?

VIV: I think so. But she should be up soon.

PARKER: I'm not here for— We should talk.

*(*VIV *shifts.)*

VIV: Oh.

PARKER: Yeah.

VIV: Look, I know we're not each other's biggest fans right now but I really am— *(just trying to help)*

*(*PARKER *throws the balled up pieces of paper on the table to interrupt* VIV.*)*

VIV: What's this?

PARKER: Read it.

VIV: *(As she's reading them)* Oh my God.

PARKER: Yeah.

VIV: This is unreal.

PARKER: That's not all of it.

VIV: Not all of—I didn't think…I thought… *(Her voice trails off.)* How long has this been happening?

PARKER: Months apparently.

VIV: This is all out harassment.

PARKER: I know. She just told me.

VIV: How did she not

We need to tell the police.

PARKER: We can't.

VIV: Why not?

PARKER: She doesn't
It's not an option okay?

VIV: This is intense. It has to be personal. This person knows her.

PARKER: Personal?

VIV: Yeah. And not like race related. Black women just aren't targeted in this way.

PARKER: In this way?

VIV: Don't try to make me seem
Yes. These sort of attacks are usually aimed at black men not—

PARKER: Black men? Are you shitting me?

VIV: I'm just saying from what I've seen—

PARKER: Could you please not be you for one second?

VIV: Parker.

PARKER: I am coming to you as one of Cass's best friends talking to the other one trying to figure out what to do. And it's not calling the police. Or planning a march. We're not calling the paper and we're not—

VIV: I didn't call the paper. I called my sister.

PARKER: This is about protecting Cass. Not ourselves. Cass. I'm trying to She needs our help.

VIV: How can I help her if she won't even talk to me? She's so…numb right now. All she wants to do is ignore it and pretend it isn't happening.

*(*PARKER *sits down and joins* VIV *at banana grams.)*

PARKER: She's…uh…not really talking to me either. *(Referring to the Banana Grams)* I'm surprised you still have these.

VIV: Yeah. From our secret Santa exchange. How did we always end up getting each other's names?

PARKER: Cass probably rigged the system. She really wanted us to be friends. *(A moment)* Maybe I should alert the campus police. Right? They've gotta be more approachable than the city. I'm just not sure how I'd tell them without

*(*CASS *enters.* PARKER *and* VIV *don't notice.)*

VIV: Without them calling the city police since this is an all out hate crime?

PARKER: Viv, you really need to—

CASS: I called Dean West this morning.

PARKER: Cass.

CASS: She agrees with me that Equality Day should be called Unity Week. We're spreading the events across a week at different times so different students can attend.

PARKER: Cass, we need to talk about—

CASS: I'll still give the keynote. But on the first day as a kick off. And then my tenure meeting, interview, whatever will be Friday. So speech on Monday, find out if I'm being fired on Friday.

PARKER: Cass.

CASS: Viv.
Is there coffee?

VIV: Cass, this is serious stuff. We're worried about—

*(*CASS *checks the time.)*

CASS: It doesn't matter. I'll be late to work anyway. Maybe I'll call in sick. I'm a little tired.

PARKER: You haven't thought this through. What if something—

CASS: Don't. *(She leaves.)*

PARKER: She's going to wait until she gets shot before she does something.

VIV: Can I call the police now?

PARKER: No. She doesn't trust the police. She'll…fuck. I shouldn't have come to…you. I was just worried. Who knows what this person will do next? I thought it was just the car. But the car and this? What if they

(There's a moment of silence.)

VIV: I'm worried that if we do nothing, if we do not involve the police

PARKER: Not now, Viv

VIV: That this will be on our hands.

PARKER: Viv, you don't—

VIV: It will be our fault when she dies. Because you didn't let me make a single step without insulting and belittling me.

PARKER: This isn't about you , Viv.

VIV: I'm not making it about me. I'm making a point. Talk to her. And do something. You're both circling around each other, waiting—

PARKER: You don't get it, Viv.

VIV: I don't need to get it right now. Right now I just need to know she'll be okay and I'm not going to just hope nothing bad happens.
Doing nothing is still making a choice and it's the wrong one.

(Shift)

PARKER: Listen. I'm going to check on Cass.

VIV: Parker, you can't just walk away from this.

PARKER: I'm walking away from you, Viv. Not this.

VIV: We need to create a safe space for her.

PARKER: There's no such thing as a safe space for people like me. Or Cass. Safe spaces are for white people. The rest of us…we're never really safe. Not really.

VIV: Your inaction is going to destroy you. You know that I am right about this.

PARKER: I'm checking on Cass. Good luck with your banana grams.

*(*PARKER *leaves.* VIV *knocks the banana grams off the table.)*

Scene 9

*(*CASS *in her office, typing on her computer. Every few moments she reaches for her coffee. There's a brick on her desk.* PARKER *enters and stands by the door.)*

PARKER: Your car isn't in the parking lot.

CASS: I had it towed out.

PARKER: At what point are we going to start treating this problem like it's a real problem?

*(*CASS *doesn't stop working.)*

PARKER: Have you told the campus police?

CASS: Nope.

PARKER: Cass, you have to say something. I'm serious. And I know that—

CASS: What do you think happened?

PARKER: What?

CASS: What do you think happened? To my car

PARKER: There's a brick on your desk.

CASS: Pick it up.

*(*PARKER *picks up the brick and reads it. The brick say "Love."* PARKER *looks up at* CASS *confused.)*

CASS: My idea. We're going to "build a wall" but a wall of love. I did a small preview for Dean West this morning and she loved it. She went to buy the brick today. During Unity Week, students will be able to—

PARKER: Yeah. I got it. So your car isn't in the parking lot because?

CASS: A student hit it when she was trying to get out of a parking spot.

PARKER: Cass

CASS: And before you turn this into some sort of racist conspiracy against me, I watched her hit my car. She was just a bad driver.

*(*PARKER *sits down.)*

PARKER: Any new notes today?

*(*CASS *shakes her head.)*

PARKER: Have you told anyone about those?

CASS: Why? So we can have No Hate November? Another event I'll have to plan. No thanks.

PARKER: People should—

CASS: You've made your point Parker. *(She moves from the computer and looks for a file.)*

(Pause)

PARKER: When I first moved here, I didn't tell anyone I was trans. Didn't have to.

CASS: K.

PARKER: You were one of the first people I told.

CASS: Yup. I remember. I was also there.

PARKER: Cass, could you--could you stop working for one minute?

(CASS *stops.)*

PARKER: Some of my students don't really know. Most of my students don't know. Faculty only knows because we all had to sit in on that diversity inclusion seminar.

(CASS *reluctantly cracks a smile.)*

CASS: Right. I forgot about that. I hate those.

PARKER: Right. So it was me, you, Akeem, and Riya all sitting together because we were like "Cool I know exactly how this is going to go down." When they talked about black people

CASS: Oh. Ugh. Everyone just kept staring at me.

PARKER: When they got to Asian Americans, they all stared at Riya. Religious inclusion was time to stare at Akeem

CASS: And then when they got to trans people Dean West was talking directly to you

PARKER: And then everyone else was staring at me remember?

CASS: That's how they all found out?

PARKER: I got so many emails after that apologizing about their language around me.

CASS: Ew.

PARKER: Exactly. Professor O'Hara honest to God said she would begin to call herself "zir" in solidarity.

CASS: Can we officially say she sucks? She tried to tell me her great grandp arents are from South Africa so we were probably related.

PARKER: Nooooo

CASS: Yes. Actual words from her mouth.

PARKER: Geez. Anyway, so after everyone found out, I remember it just being tense whenever I walked into rooms. Like people were trying too hard to make me feel comfortable.

(CASS returns to her work.)

CASS: Okay.

PARKER: And I just knew if something happened to me, everyone would verbally be there for me. I'd get a lot of cards and nice words but

CASS: But that'd be it.

PARKER: No one gets it more than me that reporting this won't change the culture here. People will be cool for a week and then go back to their shitty selves.

CASS: If you get it, then why are you pressuring me?

PARKER: Because we're not doing this for the sake of the campus. You need to tell the police in case there's some person out there trying to hurt you. They're clearly escalating.

(Shift)

CASS: I already called the police.

PARKER: What?

CASS: About the notes. I called them. They said they'd add it to my case and would let me know if they discovered anything. But without cameras, they weren't sure how much they could do.

PARKER: Okay. So what're you going to do?

CASS: What?

PARKER: Self protection. Want me to walk with you to your car?

CASS: I don't need an escort.

(There's a knock on CASS's door.)

PARKER: You shouldn't be walking to your car alone.

CASS: Come in.

*(*DEAN WEST *enters.)*

DEAN WEST: Oh perfect. Is this a planning committee?

*(*PARKER *stares at* CASS.*)*

PARKER: Not exactly.

DEAN WEST: Well I don't mean to intrude. I just wanted to let you know how excited students are about Unity Week.

(Both PARKER *and* CASS *fake the best smiles they can.)*

DEAN WEST: I've read Mara's speech and it's actually quite aware. I'm very impressed with what she's put together.

CASS: That's great.

*(*DEAN WEST *picks up the brick.)*

DEAN WEST: *(To* PARKER*)* Is this not the best idea? When Professor Davis told me about it, I was BLOWN AWAY. With all this rhetoric of building a wall, it's such a great way to combat that.

PARKER: Yeah. It won't stop them from building an actual wall though. Like, on the border.

DEAN WEST: What?

PARKER: I mean, the wall will put good vibes out there but won't stop the building of the wall across the border.

DEAN WEST: I'd like to think one good deed can spread across the nat—

PARKER: But it can't though. The only way to stop the president from building a wall is to physically stand in the way.

DEAN WEST: Are you suggesting we send students to the border towns? They could write a paper on their experience there. I don't know how we'd ensure their safety but I'm sure we could get funding. Imagine what that'd do for awareness. You know, at my college, during Spring Break, we went down to Juarez and passed around water to people. What a brilliant idea.

*(*DEAN WEST *leaves as she continues to plan.* CASS *looks at* PARKER.*)*

CASS: See? That's exactly what will happen if I make what's happening to me obvious. She's going to get student interns to escort me to my car so they can write a research paper on race relations. Have them present it to the board and then apply for some crazy diversity grant.

PARKER: If she tries to make me go to Juarez, I'm telling her you're Dominican.

CASS: Half!

PARKER: Yeah. Half's enough to be my translator.

CASS: Parker, you really should work on your Spanish. You're Puerto Rican. Your students expect you to—

PARKER: Puerto Ricans speak shit Spanish. *(A moment. Starts laughing)*

CASS: What?

PARKER: I started to think about what event she'd plan if she heard about these notes being left in your office.

CASS: *(Trying to do* DEAN WEST*'s voice)* Let's do a letter campaign and send every teacher on campus a letter in appreciation to combat this hate.

PARKER: Let's put up letters all over the school and cover our walls with love.

CASS: *(Still mocking)* We must be the change we want to see in the world. *(Moment)* I'm still pissed at you for telling Viv.

PARKER: I know. But I had to. I'm worried.

CASS: I'm okay.

PARKER: Cass, no you're not. Do something. You can't just wait for this person to

CASS: To what? You sound like Viv.

PARKER: You keep acting like it's nothing. This person is just going to keep—

CASS: This person is a coward who is never going to make any real move.

PARKER: How "real" of a move are you looking for? What are you waiting for to happen?

(Moment)

CASS: Parker. Honestly. I'm fine. It's fine.

Scene 10

(The night before Unity week begins [Sunday night]. CASS *in her living room, reading a comic book and drinking water.* VIV *enters holding a bunch of books. She and* CASS *get eye contact.)*

CASS: Um. Hi.

VIV: Hi.

CASS: Are you about to hand me a syllabus?

VIV: Can we talk? Like honestly talk?

CASS: Um

VIV: Okay so *(She sets the books down. She pick up Collins' Black Feminist Thought.)* This is the first book I read that shattered everything I believed in. I cried for days after reading it.

CASS: Cool.

(VIV sets that book down and then picks up hooks' Killing Rage.)

VIV: This book put something in me. It made me want to be an activist. I read it while I was in grad school

CASS: Viv, I'm going to stop you because you've got about seven books over there all by black women and I'm not in the mood to talk about how just because you know who June Jordan is, that makes you somehow more "woke" than other white people.

VIV: I've dedicated my life to fighting for social justice and I just want to understand why you think that's not enough.

(Pause)

CASS: Why does it matter so much to you that I know?

VIV: Because you matter to me. *(A moment)* I've sort of always seen you as this person who saw through people's bullshit and could tell who really wanted to help and who was just doing it because it was cool. Activism is very cool now.
I know you don't believe me but I'm trying really hard to be one those people who actually cares. But it's not like there's a manual out there.
I know this! I have tried to find one. I don't know how to be there for you but I really really want to be. Not just because I still love you. Not just because you're Black. But because you're a human. And I just want to help. I feel…helpless. Like there's nothing I can do and I hate that.

(Moment. Can CASS trust VIV?)

CASS: My side view mirror was smashed in today. The passenger side one. And my windshield. Someone just like, went to town on my car.

*(*VIV *pulls out her cell phone.)*

CASS: What are you doing?

VIV: I'm calling the police.

*(*CASS *grabs the phone and throws it.)*

VIV: Cass!

CASS: It's fine. I throw my phone all the time.

VIV: I'm not worried about the phone.

CASS: Well I definitely don't need you to be worried about me.

VIV: If I don't, who will? You're obviously not okay.

CASS: I'm fine.

VIV: No, you're ignoring the problem.

CASS: I'm not ignoring anything.
And—what—days ago, you told me you were worried about your own safety? This isn't about me. It's been about you this whole time and your—

VIV: Cass, don't—

CASS: Can you please finally admit you called Gemma on purpose?

VIV: What?

CASS: Just admit it. You called Gemma because you wanted it in the newspaper because you wanted this to be your big moment, the next big cause you add to your long confusing list—

VIV: That's not why I did it!

(Moment)

CASS: Do you realize that everything that's happening to me right now is your fault? Because you decided to take a story that wasn't yours and make a spectacle of it?

VIV: I wasn't making a spectacle of it. I was just trying to—

CASS: To what? To force me into action? Jesus Viv. Are you really that self-involved? How did you think this would play out? Were you hoping maybe they'd put you in the newspaper and then you could talk about—

VIV: I thought she'd write something small and then it would push you into action.

CASS: Push me?

VIV: Yes! What was I supposed to do? Sit around and wait for them to— *(to murder you)*

CASS: Well you definitely made it a lot easier for them to find me.

(Moment. It's tense.)

VIV: I'm going to stay with Gemma tonight. Hopefully tomorrow we can talk about this. Assuming you're not dead by then. *(She grabs her phone and car keys and then leaves the house.)*

Scene 11

(Monday afternoon. It's time for the key note. PARKER, DEAN WEST, *and* MARA *are on stage facing the audience.* VIV *is not there.)*

DEAN WEST: *(Whispering to* PARKER*)* Where is she?

PARKER: I just texted her. She should be here soon.

DEAN WEST: The president is coming. I hope she gets here before—

MARA: I could do a quick speech until she—

(CASS enters. She's wearing jeans and a black hoodie. She's holding her broken passenger side view mirror, the "love" brick, and a bunch of pieces of paper.)

DEAN WEST: Professor Davis, you look…are you changing?

CASS: No. I'm not. *(She goes to the podium.)* Welcome to Unity Week. I know, I know. The name needs some work. I was trying to figure out how I'd address you and what I'd say.
We obviously have real and painful problems not just in this country but in this city. Yes, our cute little liberal, keep it local city. *(She sets her side view mirror on the podium.)* Someone out there in the world has been targeting me. First, this person or these people sent me notes. Then, my car was scratched by a key. Then my side view mirror was broken off. With a bat I guess. And then they threw this brick into my windshield. And people kept telling me to do something. They kept saying "we're here for you" and "you should call the police."
Thing is, reporting these kinds of crimes leads to events like this. Events that do nothing but make other people feel better. And I just…I'm not really into that. The problem is that no one is listening to anyone. Not really. We're so convinced that these "incidents" are just rare occasions. They're not. They're happening every day all the time.
Listen I am not…or at least I'm not interested in being the poster child for "the end of racism" Or how we're all equal. We aren't. We have never been equal. That's literally how colonialism works. But you know what doesn't help and what needs to stop? White guilt. Because look where the fuck that got us.

DEAN WEST: Professor Davis.

CASS: Stop making other people accountable for your bullshit guilt. Deal with it. Stop assuming that just because you have one black friend all of a sudden you understand racial dynamics. Stop talking at us, stop marching for us and then forgetting to invite us. Stop telling us you understand. You will never understand.

DEAN WEST: Professor Davis surely—

CASS: It's all bullshit. It really is. This event is bullshit.

*(*PARKER *tries to conceal a smile.* DEAN WEST *stands.)*

CASS: But it doesn't have to be.

*(*DEAN WEST *hesitates.)*

CASS: You have to get involved. Now. Get involved before the incident. Before the tragedy. What are you doing right now to have your voice heard? To stand up for the oppressed in this community? Before you say, "This stuff doesn't happen here" take stock. Are you calling your senators about these issues or are you just posting about it?
Be honest. Is it that you don't know what to do and feel helpless or is that you really simply just don't want to? And if it's that you don't want to, could you just admit that?

*(*CASS *leaves. The characters on stage take a moment.* DEAN WEST *nudges* PARKER. PARKER *gets up and walks to the podium, is about to say something, but leaves instead.)*

*(*MARA *approaches the podium. Lights fade as* MARA *talks. [As* MARA *talks and lights fade, it should be clear she is about to be escorted away from the podium by* DEAN WEST.*])*

MARA: Welcome to Unity Week! It is my absolute pleasure. I actually prepared a keynote speech just in case Professor Davis would find this event being too stressful which is obviously what just happened. And we can't blame her. It's a very distressing time

Scene 12

(A couple hours later)

*(*CASS *sits in her office, drinking a single of bourbon in a glass. She reaches in her desk for a cigarette. Right before she can light it, the door flies open.)*

MARA: Hi Cass.

CASS: Mara? *(She takes the cigarette out of her mouth and trashes it. She looks at the bourbon. No. The bourbon can stay.)*

MARA: *(To* CASS*)* I need to talk to…you.

CASS: I'm incredibly uninterested in that.

MARA: It'll just take a minute.

CASS: Uh huh. But I said no.

*(*CASS *and* MARA *are at a stand-still.)*

CASS: What do you want, Mara?

MARA: Can I *(sit down)*

CASS: Sure.

*(*MARA *sits down and looks around the office.* CASS *waits.)*

MARA: Do you know who Trent Rhodes is?

Sorry I assumed because he was also…never mind. Trent Rhodes is an African-American student in my—

CASS: Mara, listen, I'm not exactly

MARA: But he just pulled me aside and told me sometimes my behavior is triggering.

CASS: O-kay.

MARA: I genuinely believe my calling in life is to help people. So teach me how to help.

CASS: No.

MARA: What?

CASS: Once again, I said no. Were you listening to my speech at all?

MARA: But that's what made me want to come and ask you for help.

CASS: Mara, I'm not interested in being the magical negro in your story of growth and redemption.

MARA: Professor—

CASS: And if you don't know what that very common trope is and what it means, you definitely should've taken Dr. Greene's class first.

MARA: But I—

CASS: I've had a long day, Mara.

MARA: I'm reaching out.

CASS: Not to me you aren't.

MARA: I'm trying to—

CASS: Mara, I do not have to teach you anything. I'm entitled to make my own decisions just like you're entitled to yours. And quite frankly your decisions have consequences.

MARA: But we've been on this journey together.

CASS: This journey?

MARA: I just think that—

CASS: When you decided to wear that hijab, did it ever occur to you that maybe you should talk to someone first? Or better, yet listen?

MARA: But I lead—

CASS: That's not the same thing as listening.

MARA: Well, what am I supposed to do? Have a listening party?

(CASS drinks. A moment)

CASS: I'm really not in the mood for—this.

MARA: But I'm trying to reach out.

CASS: Whether I want to help or not right?

(A moment. MARA *maybe gets it.* CASS *pulls out a piece of paper. She writes something down and hands it to* MARA.*)*

MARA: Vivienne Wilde?

CASS: She goes by Viv. Like I said, I'm no going to take this "journey" with you but if you genuinely believe your calling is helping people, you two can learn a lot from each other. Oh. And Mara. You can't keep demanding "to help", Mara. Learn how to ask.

*(*MARA *leaves.* CASS *drinks.)*

Scene 13

(That evening. CASS *is sitting in her living room, staring at the half packed boxes. Citizen by Claudia Rankine should be visible on top one of the boxes. She opens it and reads a little bit of it. There's a knock at the door. She ignores it. The door opens slightly.)*

PARKER: Is it safe to enter? Do I need to prepare an alibi and say you were with me when the house burned down?

CASS: If you were also here, how does that save either of us?

PARKER: Should I go then?

CASS: Come in, Parker.

*(*PARKER *enters with two smoothies.)*

CASS: The mango one's mine right?

*(*PARKER *nods and hands it to her.)*

CASS: No beer this time?

PARKER: Didn't feel…appropriate. What…what're you doing?

CASS: Sitting in my despair.

PARKER: So just the usual?

CASS: I'm deciding if I want to pack or not. I'd like to make one decision this week completely on my own without being forced into it.

(Moment)

PARKER: You get that email from HR?

*(*CASS *looks at* PARKER.*)*

PARKER: I'd read it to you but I deleted it as soon as I saw it. The subject line was "RE: Appropriate conduct and attire of all employees." I mean, if anything, that email is gonna backfire. I don't see Coach Sandoval showing up to baseball practice in a suit.

CASS: I've never understood how his last name is Sandoval and he's straight up Irish.

PARKER: He took his wife's last name.

CASS: Well, that's sweet.

PARKER: I think he did it to be more "relatable" to the players.

CASS: Can nothing be sweet?

(Moment)

PARKER: So, uh, do you want to talk about the speech or like your generally well-being?

CASS: My general well-being is that I am literally sitting in despair.

PARKER: But with a smoothie.

CASS: But with a smoothie.

PARKER: Dean West literally looked like she might explode.

CASS: Yeah. I'm pretty sure I'm fired.

PARKER: Nah. Probation at best. They can't afford to fire you. They just probably won't…

CASS: Tenure me.

PARKER: Yeah.

(Shift)

CASS: Why do we do it? I remember when I first started studying African American art and literature and history and I remember thinking the separatists were crazy. Like, no, running away to an all black colony is not a good idea. Like I remember someone telling me once that people who "mix the race" are just as bad as white people and I was just like "Oh my God, I thought the point was equality." And now, I dunno. Is equality even possible? Like on a minimal, minimal scale. It feels hilariously and tragically unattainable? Like not only am I black. I'm also a black woman. Which is just like…Jesus. Am I not a human? Do I not count?

PARKER: Where's Viv?

CASS: What?

PARKER: Vivienne Wilde. Pretty and crazy. Your usual type. Where is she today?

CASS: My type isn't pretty and crazy.

PARKER: It literally is.

CASS: Are you just going to ignore everything else I just said?

PARKER: I was planning on it.

CASS: She's at her sisters.

PARKER: And she asked you to be gone when she came back?

CASS: You think she's kicking me out?

PARKER: I don't think it's unreasonable to assume that. Knowing Viv.

(Moment)

CASS: When we met, she had a bumper sticker of that Yoko Ono quote. "Women are the n-word of the world."

PARKER: Hmm. Unsurprising.

CASS: Every time I see that or hear that, I think then what the hell are black women?

PARKER: Nonexistent and irrelevant apparently.

CASS: It took me three months to convince her to take that bumper sticker down.

*(*CASS *looks around at her half packed books.* PARKER *waits.)*

CASS: I have to move out, don't I?

*(*PARKER *nods.)*

CASS: It is exhausting fighting the "good fight." Don't we ever get a break?

*(*PARKER *starts to pick up books and help* CASS *pack.)*

PARKER: No. We don't. But you're not alone. And I'm sorry if I made you feel like you were. You're not. I'm here. How can I help?

*(*CASS *and* PARKER *share a sweet moment.)*

CASS: I've got a half packed box upstairs with just pants in them. I might also need shirts when I leave.

PARKER: On it. *(He starts to move upstairs.)*

CASS: And thank you for asking.

*(*PARKER *nods. He heads upstairs.* CASS *reaches for Citizen by Claudia Rankine.)*

END OF PLAY

END OF PLAY

www.ingramcontent.com/pod-product-compliance
Lightning Source LLC
LaVergne TN
LVHW050341160826
845677LV00014B/3731

* 9 7 9 8 8 8 8 5 6 0 0 5 1 *